With love, for

....

From ....

Date ....

Memories from your
Grandmother

AT THE BEGINNING

Our Family Tree

Great Grandma

Great Grandpa

Great Grandma

Great Grandpa

Grandma

Grandpa

Mother

Me, aged ....

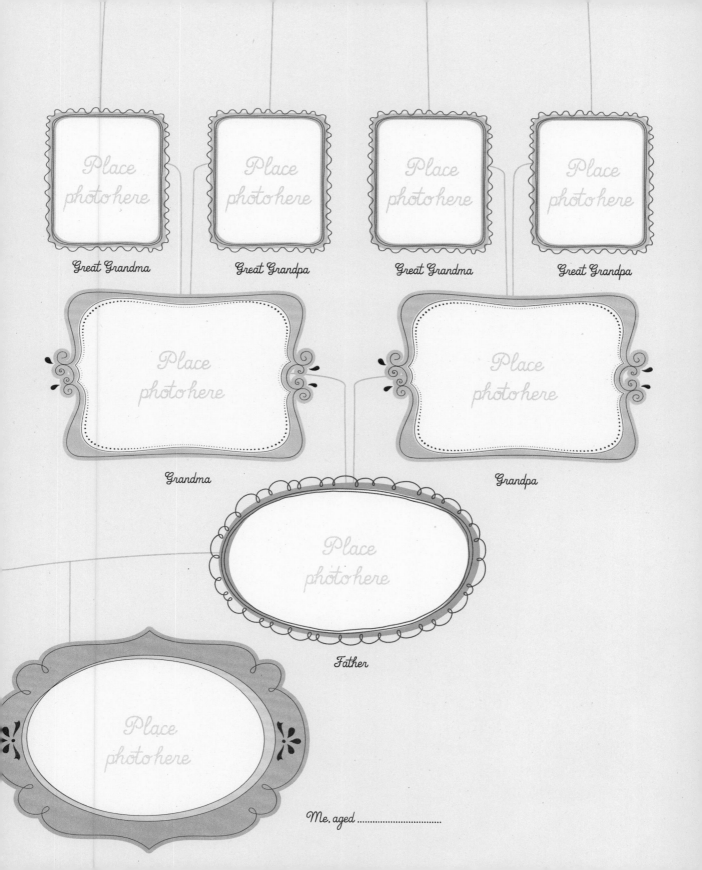

Place photo here

Great Grandma

Place photo here

Great Grandpa

Place photo here

Great Grandma

Place photo here

Great Grandpa

Place photo here

Grandma

Place photo here

Grandpa

Place photo here

Father

Place photo here

Me, aged ....

My Great-Grandparents

My Mom's Maternal Grandparents were

Grandmother .... Heritage ....

Grandfather .... Heritage ....

Their story ....

....

....

My Mom's Paternal Grandparents were

Grandmother .... Heritage ....

Grandfather .... Heritage ....

Their story ....

....

....

My Dad's Maternal Grandparents were

Grandmother .... Heritage ....

Grandfather .... Heritage ....

Their story ....

....

....

My Dad's Paternal Grandparents were

Grandmother .... Heritage ....

Grandfather .... Heritage ....

Their story ....

....

....

My Grandparents

On Mom's side

Grandpa was named ....

He was born in .... on ....

His family members were ....

....

His job was ....

Grandma was called ....

She was born in .... on ....

Her family members were ....

....

Her job was ....

On Dad's side

Grandpa was called ....

He was born in .... on ....

His family members were ....

....

His job was ....

Grandma was called ....

She was born in .... on ....

Her family members were ....

....

Her job was ....

Place photo
here

First memories

I was born on...at...

I was named..

My Mom was named..

My Dad was named..

My Mom worked as a..

....

My Dad worked as a..

....

My first address was ....

....

....

My earliest memory is ....

....

....

....

Major events that happened the year I was born were.......................................

....

....

....

....

Stories from my family

On my birth ....
....
....
....

How I was as a baby ....
....
....
....

How my mother coped with motherhood ....
....
....
....

How my father coped with fatherhood ....
....
....
....

Place photo here

This is ....

....

....

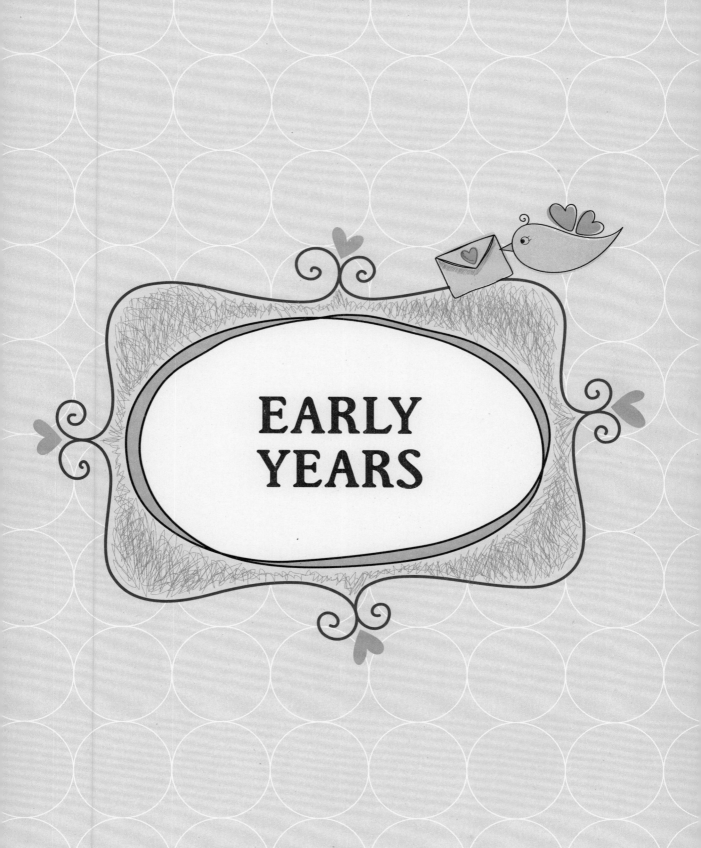

EARLY YEARS

When I was a girl...

A can of soda cost $................................

A candy bar cost $................................

A loaf of bread cost $................................

A carton of milk cost $................................

A ticket to a movie cost $................................

A good salary was about $................................

A regular car cost $................................

A family home cost $................................

A gallon of gas cost $................................

The President was ....

The most popular TV show was ....

The most popular movie star was ....

The most popular singer was ....

Elementary School Days

My first school was named ....

My favorite teacher was named ....

My friends were named ....
....

My favorite subject was ....
....

What I liked about school was ....
....
....

What I didn't like about school was ....
....
....
....

I was always getting into trouble for ....
....
....
....
....

The funniest thing that happened at school was ....
....
....
....

Place photo here

Me at school, age...

My friends

My best friends were..
....
....

We would spend our time..
....
....
....
....

The funniest thing we did was..
....
....
....

They probably would describe me as..
....
....
....
....

Place photo here

Place photo here

My Favorites as a girl

Song ....
....

Movie ....
....

TV show ....
....

Radio station ....
....

Sports ....
....

Actor ....
....

Actress ....
....

Color ....
....

Book ....
....

Food ....
....

Outfit ....
....

Place photo here

Place photo
here

A day I remember fondly

GROWING UP

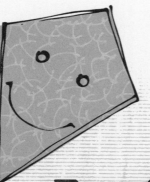

Family Vacations

A typical family vacation would be ....
....
....
....

We would often go to ....
....
....
....

My favorite vacation was to ....
....
....
....

The thing I loved to do on vacation was ....
....
....
....

Place photo
here

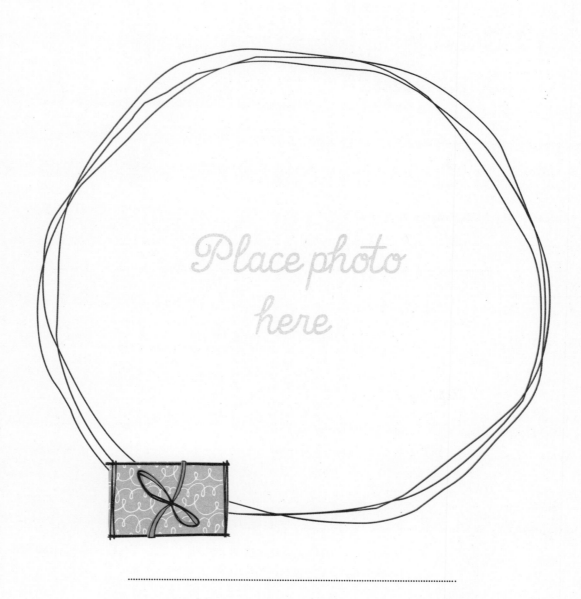

Place photo here

....
....
....

Birthday parties

In our house, birthdays we always celebrated by ....
....
....

My Mom would always make ....

One particular party I will always remember was when ....
....
....
....
....

My favorite gift was ....
....

The funniest party was when ....
....
....
....
....
....
....
....

Place photo here

High School

My high school was named ....
....
My favorite subject was ....
....
....
My favorite teacher was named ....
....
....
I was a .... kind of student
When I was in high school I wanted to be ....
....
....
....
....

Friends and Hobbies

My best friends were named ....
....
....
....

We would spend our time together ....
....
....
....
....

The hobbies we shared were ....
....
....
....
....

Place photo here

Place photo here

Place photo here

A picture of my house, taken in ....

....

....

Where I lived

My address was ....
....
....

I would describe my childhood home as ....
....
....
....
....
....
....

My favorite part of the house was ....
....
....
....
....
....

Place photo here

This is a photo of ....

Teenage Years

As a teenager, my favorite things were:

Song ....

Movie ....

TV show ....

Time of the day ....

Sports ....

Actor ....

Actress ....

Color ....

Book ....

Food ....

Outfit ....

Place photo
here

Place photo
here

INTO ADULTHOOD

Place photo here

....
....

Place photo here

....
....

After Graduation

I graduated high school on ....

After this achievement I went on to ....
....
....
....
....
....
....
....
....
....
....
....
....
....
....
....

Working 9 to 5

My first job was ....

My salary was ....

I spent my first pay check on ....

....

....

I liked working because ....

....

....

....

Although I didn't like ....

....

....

....

Working for a living taught me ....

....

....

....

....

....

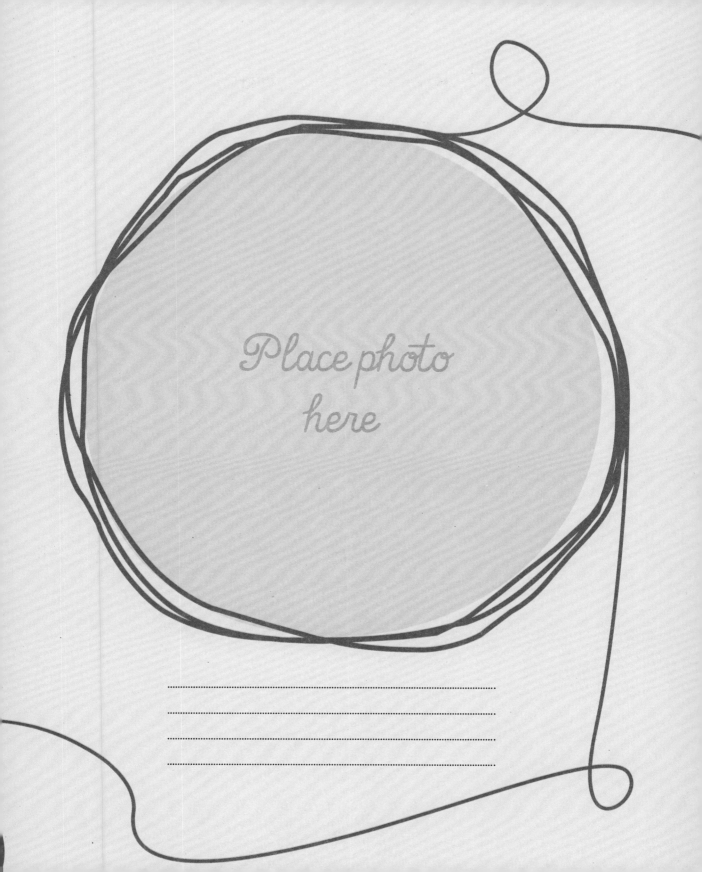

Place photo here

A day I remember fondly...

....

....

....

....

....

....

....

....

....

....

....

....

....

....

Place photo
here

Place photo
here

Place photo
here

Place photo
here

LOVE AND MARRIAGE

I first met Grandpa ....

My first thoughts were ....

....

....

When my parents first met him, they ....

....

....

While we dated, we ....

....

....

....

Back then, the thing I loved about him most was ....

....

....

....

Meeting Grandpa

Place photo here

Place photo
here

Grandpa and I were married...

Date ....

Time ....

Place ....

....

We had our reception at ....

....

....

We ate ....

....

....

....

Our first dance was ....

....

....

My dress was ....

....

....

....

Our Honeymoon

After we got married, we went on our honeymoon to ....

....

....

We traveled by ....

We were away for ....

My fondest memory is when ....

....

....

....

My favorite part of the honeymoon was when ....

....

....

....

....

....

Our First Home

Place photo here

Our first home together was at ....
....
....

We lived there for ....
....

In the first year of marriage we spent our time ....
....
....
....
....
....
....
....

The times I cherish the most are ....
....
....
....
....
....
....

Grandpa worked as a ....
....

I worked as a ....
....

A FAMILY OF MY OWN

Pregnancy and Birth

I found out I was first pregnant in ....

....

....

When I found out I felt ....

....

....

My pregnancy was ....

....

....

I loved being pregnant because ....

....

....

....

....

....

But the worst thing about being pregnant was ....

....

....

Place photo here

Place photo here

My children growing up

The thing I loved the most about being a mother back then was.......................................

....

....

....

....

....

....

....

My children loved to play..

....

....

....

....

....

....

As a family, we would ....

....

....

....

....

....

....

Family Vacation

As a family, we would go on vacation to ....

....

....

....

The children liked to ....

....

....

....

Grandpa would always ....

....

....

My favorite vacation with my family was when we went to ....

....

....

....

....

A typical vacation would be ....

....

....

....

....

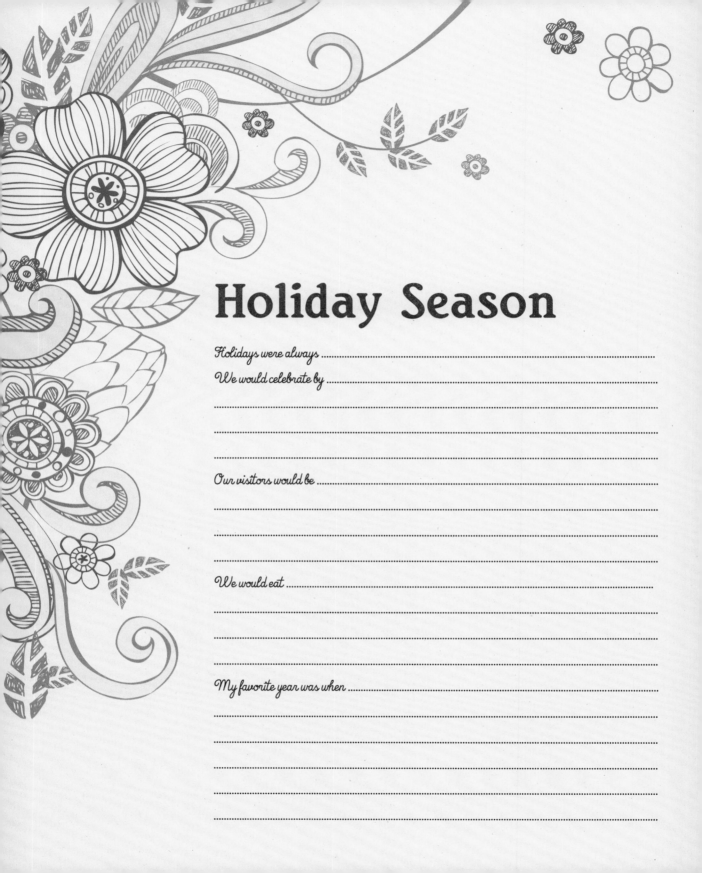

Holiday Season

Holidays were always ....

We would celebrate by ....

....

....

....

Our visitors would be ....

....

....

....

We would eat ....

....

....

....

My favorite year was when ....

....

....

....

....

....

Place photo
here

THE NEXT
STAGE

My children leaving home

My last child left home in ....

I initially felt ....

....

....

....

....

....

....

I decided I would use my time doing ....

....

....

....

Place photo
here

Place photo here

Time to ourselves

Once our children left home, we spent our time ....

....

....

....

We went on vacation by ourselves again to ....

....

....

....

We enjoyed this time because ....

....

....

....

Place photo here

By then, Grandpa worked as a ....
....

I worked as a ....
....

We spent time with our friends ....
....
....
....
....
....

My hobbies

In my spare time my hobbies are ....
....
....
....
....
....
....
....

Having hobbies is important to me because ....
....
....
....
....
....
....
....
....
....
....

Place photo
here

Place photo
here

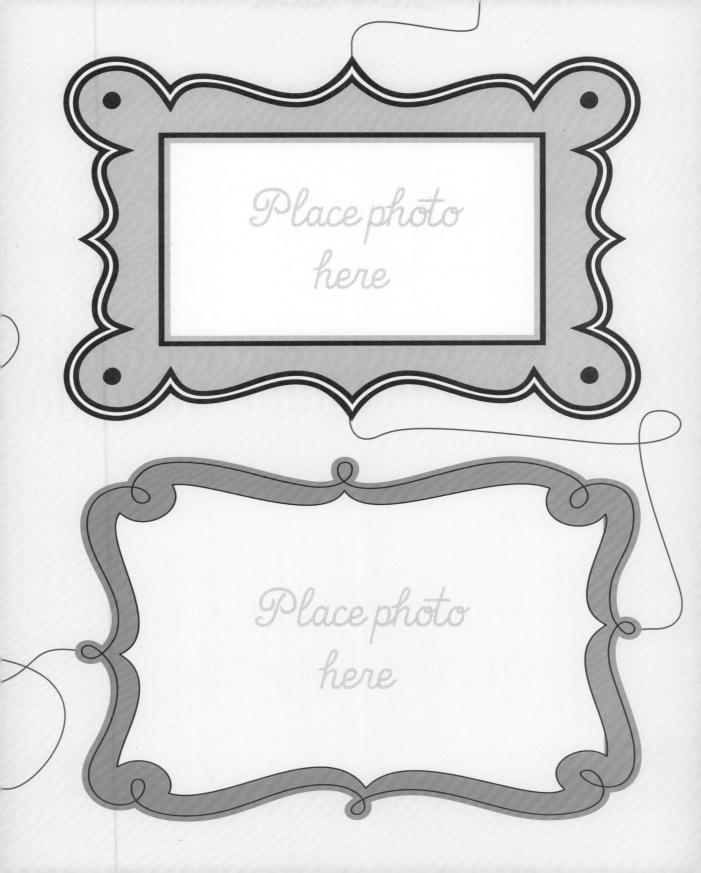

THE CIRCLE
OF LIFE

Place photo here

Place photo here

Grandchildren

My first grandchild was born

On ....

At ....

The baby was named ....

When I heard the news I ....

....

My other grandchildren are ....

....

....

....

We play ....

....

....

The thing I love about my grandchildren is ....

....

....

....

....

The best thing about being a Grandmother is ....

....

....

....

My life now...

Place photo here

My favorite things to do now are ....
....
....
....
....

My favorite vacation places are ....
....
....
....

My favorite family memory is ....
....
....
....

If I could pass on one piece of wisdom to you it would be ....
....
....
....
....

How my life has changed

Place photo
here

Place photo
here